Exposing God Amidst the Chaos

— JAMES BARS —

Copyrights and Permissions:

Copyright to the author and quoted authors: All rights reserved, 2012

Woven throughout this work are quotations and paraphrases from the Holy Scriptures. The paraphrases often roughly resemble the language of the *New International Version*. NIV. Copyright 1973, 1978, 1984 and *The New International Version* TNIV. Copyright 2001, 2005, 2007 by the International Bible Society. Used by permission of Zondervan. All rights reserved.

Disclaimer and Warning: The information in this book is offered with the understanding that it does not contain medical, psychological, legal, financial, or any other professional advice. Individuals who require such services should consult with competent professionals. The author and publisher make no representations about the suitability of the information contained in this book for any purpose. This material is provided "as is" without warranty of any kind. Although much effort has been made to ensure the accuracy of the contents of this book, errors and omissions can occur. The author and publisher assume no responsibility for any damages arising from the use of this book, or alleged to have resulted in connection with this book. This book is not completely comprehensive. Some readers may wish to consult additional books or professionals for advice.

    Editor: Elsi Dodge - www. RVTourist.com/blog
    Beta Readers, Lowell Troyer and Suzanne Bars
    Cover design: James Bars
    Technical Supervision: Nathaniel Tainter - Golden Apples Design
    Drawing of Jesus: Kip Ayers - www.kipayersillustration.com
    Initial Publication Date: 1-19-2015

ISBN: 978-0-9862397-0-0

DEDICATION

This journey is dedicated to you.

May the light that reflects from these pages warm your soul and brighten the horizons of your eternal destiny.

A large percentage of the author's proceeds

are divided equally among the following charities.

Compassion International

Angel Tree

Child Fund International

ADRA

World Vision

Please join us in providing for the needs of God's children around the world. Select a charity and give. Give of yourself and you will find joy. Jesus said that when we do things for His children in need, it is as if we were doing them for Him. Let us store our treasures in Heaven.

"Come to me, all you who are weary and burdened, and I will give you rest. Take my yoke upon you and learn from me, for I am gentle and humble in heart, and you will find rest for your souls." *Matthew 11:28-29 NIV*

TABLE OF CONTENTS

Chapter One: Who Is Your God? And, Why The Chaos?..6

Chapter Two: Lies Or Laws?........................9

Chapter Three: God Is Angry For You—Not At You 12

Chapter Four: Hell, No 15

Chapter Five: Good vs. Evil—Who is Responsible......21

Chapter Six: The War Begins 25

Chapter Seven: Fear Or Love? 28

Chapter Eight: Angry Love?......................31

Chapter Nine: Your Choice.......................35

Chapter Ten: The Spirit Arrives—The Big Bang 41

Chapter Eleven: The Death Trap 44

Chapter Twelve: How Do I Look?..................47

Chapter Thirteen: John 3:16—The Way Home........51

Chapter Fourteen: Promises 57

Notes..63

Chapter One

Who Is Your God?

And, Why the Chaos?

    Whose picture of God do you see? Through what lens do you view Him? Is He love? Is He vengeful? Is He full of wrath and fury? Is He distant, arbitrary and punishing? Is He close, personal and caring?
How did you come to your current view of God? Can you trust your sources?
    Why is it important to have a correct understanding of who God is? Believe it or not—your beliefs about your Creator will either enhance or distort your every motive, affection, desire, feeling, action and thought throughout your entire life.
    Your personal understanding of God's character affects your health, your happiness, your peace, and your joy, as well as your productivity and ability to cope with the struggles of life on a difficult, dangerous and rebellious planet.
    A chief purpose in putting this book together is to reflect onto

Chapter One / *Who Is Your God? And, Why the Chaos?*

God's true character the light of His love that currently illuminates our hearts. We wish to demonstrate that He is love, and that He desires you. He longs to restore you and have you realize the intensity of His passion for your advancement in this world and the next. Beyond a shadow of doubt, know this—He is completely devoted to your success and wholeheartedly loves and cares for you.

Concerning you, He said:

Can a mother forget the baby at her breast and have no compassion on the child she has borne? Though she may forget, I will not forget you!
See, I have engraved you on the palms of my hands; your walls are ever before me. Isaiah 49:15-16 NIV

For I know the plans I have for you," declares the Lord, plans to prosper you and not to harm you, plans to give you hope and a future. Jeremiah 29:11 NIV

The depths of God's love for you cannot be fathomed or measured. Never will any being have the capacity to love another as God loves you.

We wish to echo the sureness of His love for you and encourage the awakening of your soul to the many benefits He has granted you. Our desire is that He will enlighten, excite, and empower you to enjoy and grow in the physical, mental, emotional, and spiritual gifts He has given you.

May the truth of God's character and love inspire and enable you to accept His saving grace. May you live as happily, joyously and freely as possible while here on earth and eternally in His wonder-filled paradise.

Perhaps the best place to begin revealing why much of the world views our gracious God through a distorted lens is at the beginning, or before our beginning—before time—before the rebellion.

Before time and distance began, at least as we currently experience them, perfect harmony echoed through every pulse of life in God's creation.

No discord, dissension, or dark lies from the evil one had

marred the perfect joys of existence. All was bliss. Love and trust permeated the intelligent, eternal beings in all of God's realm. Order, logic, and reason, motivated every selfless, other-centered thought and action in the economy of His limitless domain.

But then, the great deceiver's heart of darkness began to beat with pride and rebellion. Lucifer willingly plunged into the black hole of chaos and shattered the harmony of God's selfless, love-based universe.

Chapter Two

Lies Or Laws?

Exposing fraud is often a difficult endeavour. If it could be easily seen it wouldn't be so readily used to deceive intelligent beings. Have you ever been to a magic show? Things seem to happen that you know can't happen. But they appear real. Have you ever been disappointed by someone you trusted? Someone who placed his or her own needs above yours? Someone who led you to believe they were concerned for you but as it turned out, their true motive was to get only what they wanted regardless of how you were affected.

We have a great deceiver in our midst! His name you know. His lies you have experienced. The pain he inflicts—you have felt. His deceptions have crushed the light and life out of many beautiful souls. His purpose is . . . *"To steal, to kill and to destroy."*
John 10:10 NIV

He was the most honored created being in the courts of the Father's benevolent government. He stood in the presence of the

Father and the Son, our Creator—Jesus. The anarchist's name meant *"Light Bearer or Morning Star."* Isaiah 14:12 NIV

He was dubbed, "Lucifer."

He walked in nobility of character. He was admired, trusted, loved. His beauty excelled that of all others in the kingdom. His rank among the inhabitants in the home of perfect bliss was—chief above all. He was placed above all created beings. Lucifer was made, perfect! Ezekiel 28:14-15 NIV

Before Lucifer chose to travel down the path of duplicity—all inhabitants of heaven were vibrant and alive as they operated in unison under the simple, right and true laws of the kingdom of light.

Throughout the entire universe there did not exist any discord, everyone operated in uninterrupted harmony, peace, security, safety and love. There were no shortages or loss because there were no selfish, greedy desires. A symphony of light and love beamed through each and every being as the life enhancing joy of the Creator vibrated in all and through all. This universe was built upon the sure foundation of love, for God is love. All His thoughts and actions are born from His great heart of love.

Love can only flourish in an atmosphere of absolute freedom. It cannot be coerced. It cannot be demanded. It cannot be purchased. It can only be given freely.

It is because of their great love that the Father and the Son established the laws of love and bestowed upon every created being the right to freely obey or reject the guiding principles of their kingdom. He grants free will to all.

Every kingdom, every nation, every family, every organization of any kind has its laws, its rules, its expectations, its rights of membership.

The right to belong freely to any organization is granted as long as one is willing to abide by the laws of that organization.

Laws are generally established to allow the members of an organization to operate in a known, safe environment. They are designed to ensure the thriving survival of each individual and the organization as a whole.

All of God's laws of love are designed to function in perfect harmony. Discords screech through His universal eco-system when any portion of His operating system is violated. Regardless

Chapter Two / Lies or Laws?

of whether the violations involved His physical laws of creation, His relationship laws, or His laws of love and liberty—the resulting discords sour all.

Living by God's design, you will enjoy a state of nearly constant peace with others, peace within, and peace with Him, that expands harmoniously with each new sunrise. You will experience the thrilling freedoms and joys found in living protected by God's beneficial laws of love and liberty. You will comprehend what the psalmist did concerning the amazing treasures available to mankind through the gift of surrender to our Creator's laws. It is written:

> *The law of the LORD is perfect, refreshing the soul.*
> *The statutes of the LORD are trustworthy, making wise the simple.*
> *The precepts of the LORD are right, giving joy to the heart.*
> *The commands of the LORD are radiant, giving light to the eyes.*
> *The fear of the LORD is pure, enduring forever.*
> *The decrees of the LORD are firm, and all of them are righteous.*
> *They are more precious than gold, than much pure gold; they are sweeter than honey, than honey from the honeycomb.*
> *By them your servant is warned; in keeping them there is great reward.* Psalm 19:7-1 NIV

God's universe is designed to harmonize in a perfect symphony of selfless, love-based interdependence and coexistence. When any member of the orchestra is off key, perfect unison fails, disruption slices across the sweet music and noise rips at the fabric of His creative work. Without complete obedience to the maestro's cadence and direction, the sound of His music becomes a lawless cacophony that squeals and clashes through every participant being.

Without law and order there is no harmony, no freedom, no safety, no security, no foundation, no trust, no beauty.

When all are not following the conductor, the sweetest music dies.

Chapter Three

God Is Angry For You— Not At You

Suppose a father's children are facing a double danger. Suppose they are infected with a deadly virus and there is a consuming fire heading straight for them. The father strongly warns his children to take action to avoid their destruction. The father does this out of love and concern for the safety of his children, not to restrict or withhold anything good from them. He knows, if his precious children don't take proper measures, they will die and the fire will consume them. They will all suffer. The children will suffer and the father will suffer also, because his father's heart of love wants the best for his dear ones. He longs to protect them from any harm, damage, loss or grief. He desires only joy, safety, peace and happiness for his precious children.

But the children ignore him. So, the father takes action—he provides the antidote for their disease and a vehicle to secure their safe rescue. But his children are stiff-necked and choose to continue to rebel, they ignore his warnings, deny the danger,

Chapter Three / *God Is Angry For You—Not At You*

refuse to be saved and willingly run toward the fire. Will that father possibly be hurt, saddened and angry? Will he suffer loss and grief? Yes. He will be deeply wounded at the avoidable loss of his beautiful children. But what else could he do?

God has been portrayed, by the enemy of souls, as a Father who gets angry with His children for being born into a world diseased with rebellious, self-centeredness. The enemy has portrayed God as a Father who is not only angry with them for being broken, but threatening to burn them forever if they don't love and obey Him. Is it possible that the evil one has caused a misinterpretation of Scripture in an attempt to distort God's character so that God is perceived in fearful ways? Who would willingly seek a God they are afraid of? Who wouldn't shy away from a God they believed was anxious to burn them forever?

The doctrine of souls eternally burning in hell is one of the greatest weapons devised by the enemy of your soul. It is designed to keep you distant from the Father God who loves you and wants to heal you—not punish you.

Does this concept of never ending punishment even make sense? If your children were born with a serious disease through no fault of their own, would you show your love for them by threatening them with a never ending punishment? If they were unable heal themselves and love and obey you properly would you put them in a place where the pain would never ever end? Does that sound like love?

More and more, people are beginning to question this perception of God. More and more, people are coming to understand that God is not saying, "Love and fear me or I'll never stop burning you."

God is saying, "You were born with a deadly disease—let me heal you. There is a fire coming, let me rescue you. I have provided an antidote and a vehicle for your safe return, won't you take it? Won't you let me restore you and lead you to a safe haven."

What if the fearsome, cruel picture of God that many portray was thrust upon us through our own fear-based delusions? What if sin, shame and guilt in us, has separated from God so far that we can't even imagine how gracious, compassionate, forgiving, kind and loving He is?

Didn't Adam and Eve walk face to face with God in the Garden of Eden? Yes, they did. They enjoyed His warm, happy presence. But as soon as they sinned, they hid themselves from him. Did God change or did they? It was their rebellion that brought them fear—God was not angry. He felt compassion for their loss and provided a means of redeeming the entire human race from the consequences of rebellion and sin.

What if God isn't angry at you, but angry for you? What if He isn't angry at your rebellious heart, but angry that you must suffer the curse of being born with, and live with, a rebellious heart? What if He is, what He claims to be—love?

Consider this revelation from the psalmist: *"Lord, if you kept a record of our sins, who, O Lord, could ever survive? But you offer forgiveness, that we might learn to fear you."* Psalm 130:3-4 NLT

What are Bible writers implying when they say to fear God? They are not saying to be afraid of Him. They are telling you to hold Him in high esteem, reverence and awe.

Moses, like Adam and Eve, also walked with God. On Mount Sinai, as God was delivering to him the great laws of love and liberty, He spoke His name. Moses then recorded God's name for all of us to hear: *"The LORD, the LORD, the compassionate and gracious God, slow to anger, abounding in love and faithfulness, maintaining love to thousands, and forgiving wickedness, rebellion and sin.'"* Exodus 34:6-7 NIV

Does this sound like a Father God who is angry at His broken children? Or does this sound like a Father God who wishes to forgive, heal and rescue His children from their disease and the consuming fire that will eliminate it?

Chapter Four

Hell, No

There are those who will choose to continue in rebellion and refuse God's unconditional offer. Many will justify their actions by blaming Him for the troubles and trials in their lives. Many are infected with inherited and cultivated false beliefs and misconceptions about our precious, Father God. They won't seek the truth. It will prove to be their worst decision.

Many will be misled by a false portrayal of God and turn from Him in disgust saying, "Who wants anything to do with a God who would burn them forever if they don't love and obey Him." What if it's all a lie? Who would benefit from this type of misconception concerning God? Who wants to destroy the image of God in His children's eyes? That's right—the dark one. He is a liar and the father of lies. What if he has indeed perverted the truth about God to steer souls away from seeking salvation?

What if hell is indeed the Lake of fiery, burning sulfur, discussed in Revelation 19 and 20, where the beast, the false prophet, the devil, death and Hades, and all whose names are not written in the Book of Life, are thrown? What if hell isn't a permanent fire, but a fire that purifies—permanently?

Since the fall of Adam and Eve, all mankind has known that we are desperately broken. And like Adam and Eve, our inherent shame and guilt may cause us to be afraid of God. Like a disobedient child who may be afraid of his parent, even though he knows that his parent loves him. He is afraid because he fears punishment and is overwhelmed by shame and guilt.

Could the following words from John true? It is written:

> *God is love. Whoever lives in love lives in God, and God in them. This is how love is made complete among us so that we will have confidence on the day of judgment: In this world we are like Jesus. There is no fear in love. But perfect love drives out fear, because fear has to do with punishment. The one who fears is not made perfect in love.*
> 1 John 16-18 NIV

Is God really love? We say yes! Are those who fear Him simply overwhelmed by shame and guilt and being prevented from living in love? Are you?

What if these famous words of Jesus are true?

> *For God so loved the world that he gave his one and only Son, that whoever believes in him shall not perish but have eternal life.* John 3:16 NIV

What if John's words in Revelation are true?

> *When the thousand years are over, Satan will be released from his prison and will go out to deceive the nations in the four corners of the earth—Gog and Magog—and to gather them for battle. In number they are like the sand on the seashore. They marched across the breadth of the earth and surrounded the camp of God's people, the city he loves. But fire came down from heaven and devoured them. And the devil, who deceived them, was thrown into the lake of burning sulfur, where the beast and the false prophet had been thrown. They will be tormented day and night for ever and ever. Then I saw a great white throne and him who*

Chapter Four / Hell, No

was seated on it. The earth and the heavens fled from his presence, and there was no place for them. And I saw the dead, great and small, standing before the throne, and books were opened. Another book was opened, which is the book of life. The dead were judged according to what they had done as recorded in the books. The sea gave up the dead that were in it, and death and Hades gave up the dead that were in them, and each person was judged according to what they had done. Then death and Hades were thrown into the lake of fire. The lake of fire is the second death. Anyone whose name was not found written in the book of life was thrown into the lake of fire. Revelation 20:7-15 NIV

What if the forever and ever, mentioned here in Revelation is a colloquialism—like "His sermon went on forever." Or, what if this forever, is like the forever mentioned by Jonah after he was freed from the whale.

The engulfing waters threatened me, the deep surrounded me; seaweed was wrapped around my head. To the roots of the mountains I sank down; the earth beneath barred me in forever. But you, LORD my God, brought my life up from the pit. Jonah 2:5-6 NIV

And, what if the lake of fire discussed in Revelation is the same fire mentioned by Jude when he talked about those from Sodom and Gormorrah who refused to turn from sexual immorality and perversion.

In a similar way, Sodom and Gomorrah and the surrounding towns gave themselves up to sexual immorality and perversion. They serve as an example of those who suffer the punishment of eternal fire. Jude 1:7 NIV

If Sodom and Gomorrah is an example of those who suffer the punishment of eternal fire, are they still burning? Is Jonah forever in the belly of the whale? Could a God of love, torment, torture and burn His children forever? Do you want to spend eternity with a God like that? Could you logically enjoy one day in heaven with a God who was burning people that you loved—just because they didn't want to be with Him?

What if Jesus' words are true—*"whoever believes in him shall not perish but have eternal life."* And, John's words are true, *"But fire came down from heaven and devoured them." "The lake of fire is the second death."*—It sounds like God is giving those who wouldn't be happy in His kingdom of love and light a way out.

If you've perished, been devoured and experienced the second death—it sounds like you are just gone. It doesn't sound like you are transferred to another place—does it?

God will not cheat His loyal children by surrendering His kingdom of love and light to the great deceiver.

But it seems that He will allow those who choose to not be citizens of heaven, to perish. Do you see love in that process? Can you see a Father who wishes to protect the children who will accept the cure for their deadly disease from being infected by those who refuse the treatment and want to stay as they are? Do you see love in a cleansing fire that will eternally eradicate the disease of rebellious self-centered fear?

We all suffer under the lash of rebellious, self-centered fear. God, Himself, has provided the healing balm for our great wound. He came in the form of His Son, Jesus. He came to lead us out of the desert of rebellion and into the promised land. He came to lead us back to our home in heaven. God is not angry at us for being born broken. He is angry for us. He may very well become hurt and righteously angry when He loses us because we refuse His healing and rescue attempts. But it is only because He loves us so very deeply and doesn't wish that any of us perish in the coming fire.

> *The Lord is not slow in keeping his promise, as some understand slowness. Instead he is patient with you, not wanting anyone to perish, but everyone to come to repentance. But the day of the Lord will come like a thief. The heavens will disappear with a roar; the elements will be destroyed by fire, and the earth and everything done in it will be laid bare. Since everything will be destroyed in this way, what kind of people ought you to be?*
>
> *You ought to live holy and godly lives as you look forward*

Chapter Four / Hell, No

to the day of God and speed its coming. That day will bring about the destruction of the heavens by fire, and the elements will melt in the heat. But in keeping with his promise we are looking forward to a new heaven and a new earth, where righteousness dwells. So then, dear friends, since you are looking forward to this, make every effort to be found spotless, blameless and at peace with him. [2 Peter 3:9-14 NIV]

Consider King David's revelations concerning our wonderful, Father God and the praise due Him:

Praise the LORD, my soul; all my inmost being, praise his holy name. Praise the LORD, my soul, and forget not all his benefits—who forgives all your sins and heals all your diseases, who redeems your life from the pit and crowns you with love and compassion, who satisfies your desires with good things so that your youth is renewed like the eagle's.

The LORD works righteousness and justice for all the oppressed. He made known his ways to Moses, his deeds to the people of Israel: The LORD is compassionate and gracious, slow to anger, abounding in love. He will not always accuse, nor will he harbor his anger forever; he does not treat us as our sins deserve or repay us according to our iniquities. For as high as the heavens are above the earth, so great is his love for those who fear him; as far as the east is from the west, so far has he removed our transgressions from us.

As a father has compassion on his children, so the LORD has compassion on those who fear him; for he knows how we are formed, he remembers that we are dust. The life of mortals is like grass, they flourish like a flower of the field; the wind blows over it and it is gone, and its place remembers it no more. But from everlasting to everlasting the LORD's love is with those who fear him, and his righteousness with their children's children—with those who keep his covenant and remember to obey his precepts. The LORD has established his throne in heaven, and his kingdom rules over all. [Psalm 103:1-19 NIV]

This is a picture of God worth keeping. Hang on to His love, allow Him to heal, restore and rescue you. He offers His redemption freely, just like His love. *"For God so loved the world that he gave his one and only Son, that whoever believes in him shall not perish but have eternal life."* John 3:16 NIV

Chapter Five

Good vs. Evil

Who is Responsible?

Jesus—also named Emmanuel, which means—God is with us—came to earth as one of us. He came to reveal the truth about the Father to you. As Jesus was trying to comfort His disciples, just before He endured the greatest sacrifice ever born. The sacrifice that gives you hope and reveals the depth of God's love for you. Just before He was taken away, this conversation took place:

> Thomas said to him, "Lord, we don't know where you are going, so how can we know the way?"
> Jesus answered, "I am the way and the truth and the life. No one comes to the Father except through me. If you really know me, you will know my Father as well. From now on, you do know him and have seen him."

> *Philip said, "Lord, show us the Father and that will be enough for us."*
> *Jesus answered: "Don't you know me, Philip, even after I have been among you such a long time? Anyone who has seen me has seen the Father.* John 14:5-9 NIV

Jesus has revealed the character of your Father God to you. He has blazed a trail through this dark world and offers you the same trust He offered to His disciples. *"Come follow me."* Mark 1: 7 NIV

He has summarized the selfless path you are to follow by exposing the essence of God's perfect laws of love:

> *Love the Lord your God with all your heart and with all your soul and with all your mind. This is the first and greatest commandment. And the second is like it: 'Love your neighbor as yourself.' All the Law and the Prophets hang on these two commandments.* Matt 22:37-40 NIV

This world is in a chaotic state. Don't get lost in its troubles. Focus on the simplicity of following Jesus toward home. Be obedient to loves call. He cares for you. His laws of love prove it.

Responsible parents will create a body of rules to help keep their children safe. Any caring government will do the same for its citizens. The Father and the Son were the first to do this. They diligently designed and established the laws of love to protect their loved ones and enhance their lives.

When all faithfully operate within these laws, there is love, joy, peace, safety, growth, contentment, trust, guaranteed freedom, and harmony. When the law is broken, there is fear, uncertainty, discord, discontentment, distrust and unbridled bondage.

Harmony in the kingdom of light was lost. It was lost when the great rebel, Lucifer, chose to violate the laws of love.

How could this happen? Rebellious, self-centered pride is where it all began. Lucifer's dark rebellion began with a subtle admiration of himself.

He was the most exalted among all created beings. He was beautiful beyond description, perfect in all aspects of his being. He was intelligent above all others except God. He served the countless inhabitants of the kingdom.

Chapter Five / *Good vs Evil—Who Is Responsible?*

He stood beside the throne of the Almighty.

He was God's gift! But he fell from the heights of heaven to the depths of being the most disgusting and vile creature in all creation. All this, because he lost sight of who God truly is. He lost the vision. He began to covet and crave the praise due to God alone. His heart traveled inward toward self-centeredness and far from the sure way of love. He desired to place his throne above the Father's and above the throne of the One who gave him life— the Creator—Jesus.

Pride may be the most insidious offense among all the ways to violate the heart of God's vision for His created beings. It seems that pride can find a way to justify any dark thought or action. All selfishness can be traced back to this most dangerous vacuum, this sink hole, this backwater eddy where life is sucked away and love is drowned.

Lucifer is the father of lies. They all began with pride. He no longer wished to bring glory to the Father. He wanted it for himself. He said in his dark heart. *"I will place my throne above all thrones. I will be like the Most High."* Isaiah 14:13-14 NIV

His desire was to usurp the government of heaven. His heart of darkness would no longer subject itself to the light of love. He turned away.

God in His great mercy offered Lucifer repeated opportunities to turn from the path of death. Again and again repentance and submission were presented to the great deceiver as his hope of life—he wouldn't listen. Jesus warned and counseled him. These actions only caused Lucifer to commit more allegiance to himself and his traitorous path. He had many chances to withdraw from the terrible pit, yet pride would not allow him to retreat. His course was set. His mastermind was locked firmly against the truth. He would have it all or he would have nothing. He will have nothing. Ezekiel 28 16-19 NIV

As you know—good will always triumph over evil. 1 John 3:8 NIV, Colossians 2:11-15 NIV, Hebrews 2:14-18 NIV

Love never fails. 1 Corinthians 13:8 NIV

The story was told before it began. There is nothing better for all created beings than what the Father has freely provided. He knows all.

Denial of truth, cultivation of pride, justification,

rationalization, self-righteousness, greed, hatred, lust, envy—these fruits are produced when a soul severs the cords of love.

Fear, war, destruction, heartbreak, misery, monotony, emptiness, tears, death—these are a few of the end results of prideful rebellion against the Father and His beautiful laws of love. No matter what takes place in God's domain, He takes responsibility.

Even though God did not begin the rebellion against His kingdom of love, He takes responsibility for it. Search the Scriptures and you will find Him taking responsibility for all kinds of acts that you know were not His doing. Yet, He says that He did them. He created us all. So He takes responsibility for us all.

He knows that we are not to blame for the mess we are in. Did you ask to be here? No. You just appeared one day, grew into consciousness and have been trying to figure this thing called life out, one moment at a time—one situation at a time.

Every dark deed that Satan, the father of lies, has instigated in our world, he tries to deny responsibility for and shift the blame to God. And, God takes responsibility. He has taken responsibility for each and every broken human being's mistakes. He assumes all responsibility. Not only that, He also provided a Way for you to be freed from the burdens of being born human. He did it all through Jesus—His Son.

Therefore, if anyone is in Christ, he is a new creation. The old has passed away; behold, the new has come.
2 Corinthians 5:17, ESV

God is the burden bearer. He takes responsibility. He provides healing treatment for rebellious, self-centered fear. Your job is to accept His treatment and allow Him to restore you to His original plans for you, which include: eternal love, prosperity, purpose, creative joy and peace.

Chapter Six

The War Begins

The enemy of souls began and continues his war against God by using false propaganda. False propaganda was born in Lucifer's greedy soul. It is a twisted, mind-numbing confusion designed to unsettle innocent hearts. False propaganda is often used to deliver allegations against one's enemy. To sway hearts and minds into believing a lie. To pervert the truth. To win over. To create fear. It is used to distract, to undermine, to subdue, to divert, to subvert.

Used properly it can win a battle before it even begins. Veiled, false propaganda, deception, subtle twists of the truth and outright lies would become the tools used by the great deceiver to turn the hearts embraced in love away from allegiance to the Father. Genesis 3:1-13 NIV

Before the controversy became overwhelmingly confusing, God summoned all angels into His presence and presented the truth before them so informed decisions could be made. The great deceiver twists and perverts the truth as he brings his false allegations against God.

God, however, will always be who He is—truth, love and

light. He grants freewill and intelligence to his dearly loved beings. His heart of love desires a willing allegiance; He desires no heart that is not freely offered. The most precious gift the Father could have possibly given His created beings was and is freedom. True freedom within the kingdom of light can only exist inside the framework of the laws of love.

The distortion of, and attack on, the intent behind God's law was the great weapon the first rebel, Lucifer, used to bring chaos to God's kingdom of light. He desired to rain false beliefs upon the Fathers character. Using deceit, outright lies and duplicity in a vain effort to overthrow the kingdom, he shattered the fabric of peace that, before, had enveloped each trusting heart.

The kingdom of light and the kingdom of darkness are separated by this one most significant factor—freewill.

The kingdom of light offers absolute freedom to all.

The kingdom of darkness binds beings in abject slavery.

Lucifer would imply that there was no need for the inhabitants of the kingdom of light to have laws enforced upon them. "Are not angels perfect already?" He asked.

He would attempt to lead them to believe that God's laws were designed to manipulate and control them. He would insinuate that God was withholding from them a higher level of attainment. He would try to destroy trust in the laws of love by implying that they were designed to hold the created beings back from greater and greater achievements and accomplishments. He strived to instill the belief that the laws were being used to diminish all created beings true potential. His deception was delivered in such a way that many were lead to distrust God's character and motives.

Lucifer was and is subtle, beguiling and relentless in his campaign of lies. He proposed a lawless society, a supposed state of freedom. But there can be no freedom outside the law. Any violation of God's law will always bring trouble. [Romans 6:23 NIV] It will bring trouble to the one in violation, trouble to those who must enforce the law, trouble to those who have witnessed the violation—trouble to all. [Romans 8:22-23 NIV]

Lucifer gave birth to a breach of trust that would trouble every being in the universe. It would send a rippling quake of panic, unprecedented vagary and questioning rumbling into every mind

Chapter Six / The War Begins

and heart throughout the boundless worlds. It created a sickening stench that would be dealt with.

However, this breach of trust must be dealt with in a way that would vindicate God—for in order to generate the kind of controversy needed to bring angels of the light into his dark realm, Lucifer put the Father's character on trial. Genesis 3:4-5 NIV

He accused God of forcing the allegiance of all beings into compliance to His laws. He would point to the laws of love as a violation of their freedoms, rights and privileges. He would distort their intent and cause disaffection through false propaganda, lies, distrust, flattery, any undermining means he could create and circulate from his mastermind of twisted darkness.

He began to experience a state of being heretofore unknown in all creation. He became fearful. Fear enveloped him. He had walked away from God's ways and distorted faith into fear. He liked it. He saw it as a useful tool in his campaign against the kingdom. He still does.

Chapter Seven

Fear Or Love?

God walks in faith. The enemy of souls walks in fear. All power is derived from God. The enemy must distort God's power and bend it to his use. This he achieved.

"Faith is the substance of things hoped for." Hebrews 11:1 NIV

Fear is the substance of things not desired.

Faith and fear will bring into reality that which each seeks.

In his duplicity, the enemy of truth, Lucifer, tried to appear as if he were contending for what was best for the other created beings in heaven. All the while he wove his sophistry into the fabric of peace he sought to shatter for his own benefit and no one else's.

He was allowed to proceed on his course. For if Lucifer's choices immediately resulted in his demise and that of his rebel clan before the true essence of the traitor's desires were revealed, those who remained loyal to God might do so out of fear rather than love. Love and fear cannot coexist. God is allowing the

Chapter Seven / Fear Or Love?

rebellion to play out. We will fully understand why, one day. But for now it makes sense that God is allowing the rebellion to continue until it is unquestionably revealed as unprofitable to any being—ever.

Lucifer worked slyly to gain the confidence of the angels of heaven. He felt that if he could mislead those who dwelt in the very presence of God, then those that dwelt on the outer worlds would also join him in overthrowing the kingdom.

All who joined Lucifer's rebellion were given ample opportunity to return to their previous state of peace, until the situation grew into open rebellion. Once the prince of darkness escalated his cause to the level of blatant disregard for the safety of those who remained loyal to God, then action needed to be taken to protect the remnant of the kingdom. Revelation 12:7-9 NIV

It was a devastating day, deeply wounding the hearts of the Father and the Son.

Lucifer, the most honored and privileged of all created beings in the kingdom must be torn from heaven and cast out with the train of rebels he had gathered. Grief struck deep into the very core of the Great Parent that day as He ordered the angels He loved, banished from their home.

Disappointment, emptiness, pain and loss wait at the end of all selfish ambition. For selfishness is never truly satisfied.

The rebels would be banished and quarantined in the outer reaches of God's domain, where Lucifer, now stripped of his title and position, would become known as Satan.

He had treacherously launched his fear-based kingdom of darkness and bondage and would be allowed to exercise the tenets of his lawless realm in full view of all beings—for a time. This, time, we humans were born to. What a rare privilege we have been granted. We are unique in our creation and in our re-creation. No other being will ever be able to claim redemption. Just us. Now, and through the eternal ages, beyond the demise of this horribly destructive, heart-crushing rebellion, all beings will unquestionably know the truth about God and His laws of love. And we, will be personal witnesses to the saving wonders and grace of our beautiful, selfless God. Yay!

God hides nothing. His kingdom, built upon the sure foundation of love, stands exposed by the light of truth.

God is love. If you wish to see God's true character in action, study the life of Jesus as He walked upon the earth. Jesus proclaimed:

> *If you had known Me, you would have known My Father also; and from now on you know Him and have seen Him.*
> *Philip said to Him, "Lord, show us the Father, and it is sufficient for us."*
> *Jesus said to him, "Have I been with you so long, and yet you have not known Me, Philip? He who has seen Me has seen the Father; so how can you say, 'Show us the Father'? Do you not believe that I am in the Father, and the Father in Me? The words that I speak to you I do not speak on My own authority; but the Father who dwells in Me does the works.* John 14:7-19 NKJV

Satan and his agents want you to believe that God is a wrathful, vengeful, punishing Father. These character traits are not revealed in the life of Jesus. While dying on the cross, after being tortured and brutally beaten, He actually prayed for forgiveness to be bestowed upon the human death squad who were taking His life.

Which path will you follow? Fear or love?

Chapter Eight

Angry Love?

Could the "wrath of God" mentioned in the Bible not be wrath at all but the natural consequence of violating the laws that sustain life? If you participate in destructive life-style choices, you will reap negative consequences. If you willfully murder someone and suffer the death penalty for your choice—are those charged with enforcing the law being wrathful and vengeful when they bring upon you the consequence of your choice?

God is not only responsible for creating the laws of love to protect His children, He is responsible for enforcing them with mercy and compassionate grace.

He is not vengeful or wrathful. He knows the horrible situation you were born into. He doesn't wish to punish you for being born infected with a deadly disease. He wants to heal you of your infirmity and save you from the consequences of the rebellion you have found yourself in. It is not your fault that you are infected with a terminal illness. You are not to blame for being born broken. However, you are responsible to seek and accept the treatment. Jesus provided the free cure for your deadly disease. *"For the wages of sin is death, but the free gift of God is eternal life through Christ Jesus our Lord."* Romans 6:23 NLT

Nearly eight hundred years before Jesus arrived on earth to fulfill His task of saving the world, Isaiah was busy proclaiming the hope for your cure—the antidote for rebellion and its devastating effects. The cure comes through faith in God's provision alone.

Can you find the faith to believe in and accept His freely offered remedy? Has the Lord revealed the powerful antidote to you? Isaiah wondered if anyone believed the free and freeing, good news. He wrote:

> *Who has believed our message? To whom has the Lord revealed his powerful arm?*
>
> *My servant grew up in the Lord's presence like a tender green shoot, like a root in dry ground. There was nothing beautiful or majestic about his appearance, nothing to attract us to him.*
>
> *He was despised and rejected—a man of sorrows, acquainted with deepest grief. We turned our backs on him and looked the other way. He was despised, and we did not care. Yet it was our weaknesses he carried; it was our sorrows that weighed him down.*
>
> *And we thought his troubles were a punishment from God, a punishment for his own sins! But he was pierced for our rebellion, crushed for our sins. He was beaten so we could be whole. He was whipped so we could be healed.*
>
> *All of us, like sheep, have strayed away. We have left God's paths to follow our own.*
>
> *Yet the Lord laid on him the sins of us all. He was oppressed and treated harshly, yet he never said a word.*
>
> *He was led like a lamb to the slaughter. And as a sheep is silent before the shearers, he did not open his mouth.*
>
> *Unjustly condemned, he was led away. No one cared that he died without descendants, that his life was cut short in midstream.*
>
> *But he was struck down for the rebellion of my people.*

Chapter Eight / Angry Love?

He had done no wrong and had never deceived anyone. But he was buried like a criminal; he was put in a rich man's grave.

But it was the Lord's good plan to crush him and cause him grief. Yet when his life is made an offering for sin, he will have many descendants. He will enjoy a long life, and the Lord's good plan will prosper in his hands.

When he sees all that is accomplished by his anguish, he will be satisfied. And because of his experience, my righteous servant will make it possible for many to be counted righteous, for he will bear all their sins.

I will give him the honors of a victorious soldier, because he exposed himself to death. He was counted among the rebels. He bore the sins of many and interceded for rebels.
Isaiah 53:1-12 NLT

Jesus has provided the sure cure for your rebellious heart. Look to Him. Place your faith in Him. He will heal you and you will live. God has reconciled you to Him through His willing sacrifice in your stead. If He was angry at you, would He have gone through all that misery, degradation and suffering?

God's anger is not like your anger. Your anger is often the result of self-centered fear. God's anger is always righteous anger. He is angry for you. He is angry at the injustice that pervades your dark world and the suffering that you, His dearly loved child, must endure because of it. He suffers and is frustrated when His children refuse to accept His healing, saving treatments and redemption. His great heart of love refuses to let any of us go easily. Yet He will let us go—if that is our desire.

Remember, He does not wish that any should perish. *"The Lord is not slack concerning His promise, as some men count slackness, but is long-suffering toward us, not willing that any should perish, but that all should come to repentance."* 2 Peter 3:9 NLT

Is it possible that the "wrath of God" has been misunderstood? Is it possible that we may suffer needlessly because of our own unwillingness to let go of our rebellious ways?

The nation of Israel described in the Bible, we believe, is symbolic of spiritual Israel. Their story is our story. God sought to rescue and bless them with every piece of His heart, yet they would not turn and be healed.

> *Listen to me, O my people, while I give you stern warnings.*
>   *O Israel, if you would only listen to me!*
> *You must never have a foreign god; you must not bow down before a false god.*
> *For it was I, the Lord your God, who rescued you from the land of Egypt.*
>   *Open your mouth wide, and I will fill it with good things.*
> *But no, my people wouldn't listen. Israel did not want me around.*
> *So I let them follow their own stubborn desires, living according to their own ideas.*
> *Oh, that my people would listen to me!*
> *Oh, that Israel would follow me, walking in my paths!*
> Psalm 81:8-13 NLT

This plea is not coming from a vengeful, vindictive heart. It is coming from a heart of perfect love. His angry love wails at the loss of one precious soul. He came to draw His children out of the darkness and into the light. God does not want to spend eternity without any of us. But if we won't let go of the darkness—He must release us—just like ancient Israel. He offers you the ability to stand reborn, renewed, refreshed and reestablished. You can be transformed into a being who can stand in His all-consuming presence.

Chapter Nine

Your Choice

All who are not made new will not be able to exist when God returns to finish the war that Satan launched against the kingdom of light. At the end of days there will be a cleansing fire. Perhaps, not a fire that eternally punishes those broken souls who would rather not walk in the light. But a cleansing fire that allows them to perish eternally.

Those who chose to remain in rebellion will be left to reap the consequences of their stubborn desires. They won't be able to exist in His presence. The brightness of His glory will devour all darkness. *"For our God is a consuming fire."* Hebrews 12:29 NKJV

Consider these enlightening texts,

> Then I turned to see the voice that spoke with me.
> And having turned I saw seven golden lampstands, and in
> the midst of the seven lampstands One like the Son of Man,
> clothed with a garment down to the feet and girded about

the chest with a golden band. His head and hair were white like wool, as white as snow, and His eyes like a flame of fire; His feet were like fine brass, as if refined in a furnace, and His voice as the sound of many waters; He had in His right hand seven stars, out of His mouth went a sharp two-edged sword, and His countenance was like the sun shining in its strength.

And when I saw Him, I fell at His feet as dead. But He laid His right hand on me, saying to me, "Do not be afraid; I am the First and the Last. I am He who lives, and was dead, and behold, I am alive forevermore. Amen. And I have the keys of Hades and of Death. Revelation 1:12-18 NKJV

I looked when He opened the sixth seal, and behold, there was a great earthquake; and the sun became black as sackcloth of hair, and the moon became like blood.

And the stars of heaven fell to the earth, as a fig tree drops its late figs when it is shaken by a mighty wind. Then the sky receded as a scroll when it is rolled up, and every mountain and island was moved out of its place.

And the kings of the earth, the great men, the rich men, the commanders, the mighty men, every slave and every free man, hid themselves in the caves and in the rocks of the mountains, and said to the mountains and rocks, "Fall on us and hide us from the face of Him who sits on the throne and from the wrath of the Lamb! For the great day of His wrath has come, and who is able to stand?" Revelation 6:12-17 NKJV

But who can endure the day of His coming?
And who can stand when He appears?
For He is like a refiner's fire
And like launderers' soap. Malachi 3:2 NKJV

God's presence is like a lake of consuming, refining fire. Nothing impure can exist in His presence. Could it be that God's wrath is nothing more than a rebellious beings inability to stand in His presence? His eyes are like flames of fire. His face is as bright as the sun. Who can stand in His presence? He is powerful and magnificent beyond your ability to comprehend power and

Chapter Nine / *Your Choice*

magnificence.

If you know in your heart that you have rejected Him and His free offer of restoration—of course you will wish to flee when He appears in His full glory and righteousness.

What are your beliefs about God's free offer of redemption and restoration? Where did your beliefs come from?

Where did your current beliefs about the wrath of God come from? Have you verified the reliability of your information? Or, have you simply gone along with the crowd and accepted their beliefs? Do your own study. God will open your heart to the truth about Himself. He will cleanse you so that you may stand when He returns.

The impurities of gold and silver are automatically burned away in the presence of the refiners fire. The impurities of human rebellion will be automatically burned away in the refining fire of His presence. The impurities Adam and Eve brought to you as a result of their rebellion have infested your heart and denied you the privilege of standing in the physical presence of God. If you were exposed to His physical presence in your current state of existence, you would be instantly vaporized. It is not your fault.

The only way for a broken, born in rebellion, human soul to stand in the presence of God is by being shielded through faith in the saving sacrifice of Jesus and being transformed into a different type of life form. At His coming those who are dead in Christ will rise first, then those of us who are still alive will rise with them in the air. But first, we must be transformed. If not, we would cry for the mountains and rocks to fall upon us and hide us from His face. Instead of wanting to hide from Him, those who have accepted His gift of eternal life will be changed.

> *Now this I say, brethren, that flesh and blood cannot inherit the kingdom of God; nor does corruption inherit incorruption. Behold, I tell you a mystery: We shall not all sleep, but we shall all be changed—in a moment, in the twinkling of an eye, at the last trumpet. For the trumpet will sound, and the dead will be raised incorruptible, and we shall be changed. For this corruptible must put on incorruption, and this mortal must put on immortality.* [1]
> Corinthians 15: 50-53 NKJV

Before you can stand in God's presence you must be made incorruptible and immortal. This is the last step in your transformation process. It is an actual shedding of flesh and blood and conversion into a being who bears no trace of darkness or impurity. Those who accept the gift of God through faith in Jesus Christ will experience this final stage of transformation. They will enjoy the ability to freely exist in God's presence without being vaporized.

It is a natural law of the universe—like gravity. As a human, if you step off a three thousand foot cliff without a parachute you will die. As a human, if you enter God's presence without being changed in into an incorruptible, immortal life form, you will perish.

God is not vengeful and wrathful. It is a simple truth—you were born into darkness. Darkness cannot exist in the light. Come into the light. Expose your darkness to the light and it will be vanquished.

God is not angry with you because you are broken. God is angry because you must endure the challenges of being broken. He is angry about the injustice of your situation and longs to free you from its consequences. He may feel frustrated, in the midst of heartache, when His dearly loved children refuse His offers of salvation, sanctification and restoration. His anger is always righteous anger. His heart burns at the suffering heaped upon His beautiful children as a result of rebellion and sin.

God has done everything in His power to grant you the opportunity to be transformed, but you must freely accept it. He will not force you to be with Him. He will draw you to Him through His great heart of love and willingness to bear all your burdens. But He will not force Himself upon you. If you don't believe you would be comfortable living forever in God's kingdom of light, He will allow you to perish. He certainly wishes that you will see through the lies and deceptions of Satan and place your faith in Him.

The choice is yours. You do not need to be good enough. You cannot earn the gift. If you could, it wouldn't be a gift. Salvation is yours as you accept it, by grace, through faith. Jesus cries out for you to listen and believe.

Chapter Nine / Your Choice

> Then Jesus cried out, "Whoever believes in me does not believe in me only, but in the one who sent me. The one who looks at me is seeing the one who sent me. I have come into the world as a light, so that no one who believes in me should stay in darkness.
>
> "If anyone hears my words but does not keep them, I do not judge that person. For I did not come to judge the world, but to save the world. There is a judge for the one who rejects me and does not accept my words; the very words I have spoken will condemn them at the last day.
>
> For I did not speak on my own, but the Father who sent me commanded me to say all that I have spoken.
>
> I know that his command leads to eternal life. So whatever I say is just what the Father has told me to say."
> John 12:44-50 NIV

You decide whether to accept or reject God's free offer.

You didn't decide to be born human. You didn't choose this situation. It is not your fault. It is like civilians caught up in a war. You didn't create the war, you are just caught in the middle of it. Jesus is drawing you and you know it. He said, *"And I, when I am lifted up from the earth, will draw all people to myself."* John 12:32 NIV

There is a way out for you, but you must choose to accept it— by faith. You will ultimately judge yourself.

The knowledge of God is readily available to every soul. His still small voice whispers and calls us all. You know when you are listening and you know when you choose to ignore God. You know every time you have chosen to reject Him. His words, that you reject, will be your judge. Thus you ultimately judge yourself. *"If anyone hears my words but does not keep them, I do not judge that person. For I did not come to judge the world, but to save the world. There is a judge for the one who rejects me and does not accept my words; the very words I have spoken will condemn them at the last day."* John 12:47-48 NIV

God does not desire that you perish. He freely provides a way home. If you decide to reject Him, He is hurt and angry over losing you, but He is not wrathful and vengeful. He is crying out for you to believe and to allow Him to draw you out of the darkness and into the light. He wants to heal and transform you so you can stand in His presence when He returns.

Satan wants you to reject God and remain in the dark. He wants you to reject God's free offers of rescue and renewal. He is God's enemy. He knows how much God loves you and wants you with Him now and forever. Satan strives to create an image of God that you will not be attracted to. Satan may even use the well-meaning, but misled, members of a church to scare you away and make God seem vengeful, mean and ugly.

Don't believe it. Go to God directly. Seek Him with all your heart and you will find Him. Listen to His still small voice within. God is love. Surrender to His love. You won't regret it.

Satan's government is built upon the useless foundation of fear. He lies, deceives, misleads, relishes dishonesty, instills doubt, craves terror and seeks the eternal destruction of every soul. He has twisted the truth about God's character, disrupted the kingdom of bliss and led hearts previously loyal, into open rebellion against God's kingdom of truth.

God is a very reasonable being. He asks us to come and reason with Him. *"Come now, let us reason together, says the LORD: though your sins are like scarlet, they shall be as white as snow; though they are red like crimson, they shall become like wool."*
Isaiah 1:18 ESV

What lies about God may be part of your belief system? Many people swore allegiance to Hitler and his Third Reich. How many, do you believe, did it because of the tender love and mercy graciously poured upon them? None! Does a wrathful, vengeful, vindictive view of God make you wish to be on His team forever? Come and reason with Him. The character of God is revealed through the earthly life of Jesus. Seek God's guidance. He will grant you wisdom, knowledge and understanding.

There was war in heaven. Satan and his rebel crowd were cast out. Jesus defeated Satan at the cross. As He was taking His last breath upon Calvary, Jesus said, *"It is finished." With that, he bowed his head and gave up his spirit."* John 19:30 NIV

The war has been won. Your task now is to plant His victorious flag over your heart and allow His Spirit to mop up any traces of rebellion remaining in you as you reveal His victory, in your soul, to the entire universe—forever. God wants you—choose Him.

Chapter Ten

The Spirit Arrives

The Big Bang

Prior to the war in the kingdom of light plans had been formulated to create and add an entirely new galaxy to God's universe. As a part of this new endeavor, a small solar system would be included. In this new system, the heart of life would dwell on the planet called Earth.

Before the Father and the Son advanced upon this enterprise their Spirit was there hovering over the waters. Genesis 1:1-2 NIV

The Father and Son are one. One in purpose. One in power. One in thought. They pervade every strand of DNA they have ever designed. But they are not alone. There is a third member of their existence. His name is Spirit. He, like them, is all and is in all.
Colossians 1:15-23 NIV, Colossians 3:5-11 NIV

The Father, Son and Spirit together are often referred to as the Godhead.

As the Father and the Son began preparations for the beginning of this new expansion, the Spirit was with them and the miracle was underway. It would take seven days from evening to evening each day to complete the project.

They had performed this creative process billions of times before in bringing forth other galaxies and solar systems. The task that seemed beyond belief, they had perfected. The most elaborate systems would come together precisely in the most effective life-generating, life-sustaining way. The most powerful source of life energy available—faith—would be used in the birthing process. All would be accomplished through the force of faith. They would speak and life would spring forth. God spoke, and bang! Life appeared! They would call things that are not as though they were, and they would be. Genesis 1:3 -2:25 NIV

In the beginning was the Word, and the Word was with God, and the Word was God. He was with God in the beginning. Through him all things were made; without him nothing was made that has been made. In Him was life, and that life was the light of all mankind. John 1:1-4 NIV

The Word of life spoke, and ... Bang! Colors, limbic systems, sub-systems, cell types, the elements, the breath of life, salvation plans, timing, flesh tones, water contents, interdependencies, habitats, molecule designs and functions, power sources, reproductive systems, instincts, sight receptors, hearing receptors, touch receptors, smell receptors, cell reproduction systems, taste receptors, brain functions, watering systems, feathers, light refraction, distances, shapes, waste recycling, bacteria, immune systems, moons, stars, densities of matter, temperatures, depth perception, flight patterns, emotional abilities, vocal chords, communication systems, time, evaporation rates, gravitational levels, speeds of light and sound, magnetic zones, oxygen producers, intrinsic love, carbon dioxide producers, adaptation abilities, mental functions, hair follicles, lung capacities, trillions upon trillions of simultaneous decisions and actions occurring nearly instantaneously. Beautiful! How wonderful are your ways. O my Lord.

Chapter Ten / The Spirit Arrives—The Big Bang

For since the creation of the world God's invisible qualities—his eternal power and divine nature—have been clearly seen, being understood from what has been made, so that people are without excuse. Romans 1:20 NIV

If you would like to experience an awe-inspiring presentation concerning the amazing creative abilities of our Great God, watch the video by Louie Giglio entitled, How Great is Our God. [B]

It is available on Youtube. It is forty one minutes long, so watch it when you have time to really enjoy it. Wow!

The title of "Creator" encompasses more than our limited understanding can begin to fathom. We may be able to understand the formation of a molecule, but what gives it life?

The Creator can explain.

We were designed by the force of love—awe-generating, unquenchable love.

Our planet sits within a galaxy so immense that it would take 330 million years for it to make one revolution and it is only one of billions upon billions of galaxies, each one brought forth by our Creator. On the sixth day of creation, man was formed from the dust of the earth and was given the breath of life. Genesis 1:26 NIV

Man was placed in charge of the planet. He was given authority over the earth. Genesis 3:1 NIV

He was granted free access to the Father and he communicated with the angels of light that traveled from home to here. He was perfect in every aspect. Also, bestowed upon him was his most treasured possession and gift—freewill.

The Father's heart can only love. He is love. Love may exist only when freely given. So man was given the freedom to accept the very best ... or to walk away.

Beaming with intelligence and perfection of character there did not exist within him any desire to violate the laws of love. He understood the generosity of his Creator and did not wish to separate himself from His love, power and beautiful presence.

Into God's spotless, new, gleaming world came the enemy of souls, that venomous snake—Satan. Genesis 3:1 NIV

Chapter Eleven

The Death Trap

God placed one limitation upon man as a test of fidelity. He informed him that he must not eat the fruit of the tree of knowledge of good and evil, else he would surely die.
Genesis 2:16-17 NIV

This—the enemy would place his focus on and use to entice man to distrust His Father God, whom he loved. Genesis 3:2-3 NIV

Devastating rip tides of loss and pain now stream from Adam and Eve's decision to believe the conspiring propaganda delivered from the smooth lips of the enemy of souls. They would lose their home, which contained the tree of life. They would lose the privilege of direct face-to-face communion with the Father.

Weeping, they were banished from their Eden home; stripped of their covering of light, they knew nakedness for the first time and were now dressed in the skin of the first dead creatures.
Genesis 3:21-24 NIV

They were wearing the hide of creatures they had loved, creatures they had named and played with. Now all other creatures shied away from them.

Chapter Eleven / The Death Trap

They were crushed. They were changed. Something was inherently different. They had turned to the dark side. A previously unknown rebellion had invaded their souls and destroyed their perfect existence.

They longed to go back. They wished to reverse their decision. "Please Father! We are bowed low in the dirt. We are so sorry. Please forgive us. We can't handle all this loss. Oh Father—what have we done?"

But there was no going back. The disease of rebellion had infected them. The healing process put into place from the foundation of the world must now be initiated. Mankind had severed the connective tissues of love and trust with God and His kingdom. They were now under the control of the dark side. In making their decision to turn away from the truth, they had surrendered their rights. Their right to dominion over the fish in the sea the birds in the air and every living creature that moves on the ground. Their right to unrestricted access to the Father and His Son, the Creator. Their right to live without fear and worry. Their right to perfect freedom. They had taken on the yoke of the enemy by giving themselves over to the lie—to the dark side. Oh no!

The evil one rejoiced that he had turned others away from loyalty to the laws of love. Now man was his. He delighted in his cunning ability to use the man's vulnerability with his mate to entice him into violation. Genesis 3:1-7 NIV

It was a dark day, the results of which we live in now. All death and destruction that occur now as regular events in our beautiful world stream from that choice. "Way to go Adam and Eve. I certainly wouldn't have chosen your path. Or would I? Or have I? And do I?"

Yes, we all do. For when our first earthly ancestors chose to distrust God and rebel, when they invited the darkness into their souls, they passed the deadly effects of violating God's laws of love on to their offspring.

You know this struggle. You have known it from the day of your first memory. It is a constant battle within your heart. It is the victory and the defeat that you experience in your soul with each and every moment that passes. It arises with nearly every choice you make. Paul's words echo this struggle:

> *So I find this law at work: Although I want to do good, evil is right there with me. For in my inner being I delight in God's law; but I see another law at work in me, waging war against the law of my mind and making me a prisoner of the law of sin at work within me.*
>
> *What a wretched man I am! Who will rescue me from this body of death? Thanks be to God, who delivers me through Jesus Christ our Lord!* Romans 7:21-26 NIV

Our first earthly ancestors, Adam and Eve, took this evil into their hearts and now, you too, are wired like them. You too, will know heart-breaking loss. You too, will surely die.

You too, will surely grieve. You too, will know hopelessness and pain and difficulty and uncertainty and confusion. You too, will plead and pray for freedom. You too, will strive, often unsuccessfully, to utilize your free will to overcome powerful, unhealthy habits and patterns. You too, will find that you are often powerless and weak. You too, will search for the light only to find it shining dimly as through obscured glass. You too, are familiar with the dark side. It colors every decision you make and tempts you to violate God's perfect laws of love. You too, know darkness. You may have a strong denial system. Your dark ways may be well disguised and protected in and impregnable shelter of denial, rationalization, justification, self-righteousness, pride and insecurity. However, your character, no matter how beautiful it appears to yourself and others, is marred by inherent rebellion.

Chapter Twelve

How Do I Look?

Take an honest look into the mirror of God's perfect laws of love—The Ten Commandments. How do you look? If your reflection is perfect—congratulations. If, however, you see flaws in your soul, then welcome to the family. You're broken like everyone else. You too, need a Savior. James admonished you to look intently in to the perfect law that brings freedom. He wrote,

> Do not merely listen to the word, and so deceive yourselves. Do what it says. Anyone who listens to the word but does not do what it says is like someone who looks at his face in a mirror and, after looking at himself, goes away and immediately forgets what he looks like. But whoever looks intently into the perfect law that gives freedom, and continues in it—not forgetting what they have heard, but doing it—they will be blessed in what they do.
>
> Those who consider themselves religious and yet do not keep a tight rein on their tongues deceive themselves, and their religion is worthless. Religion that God our Father

accepts as pure and faultless is this: to look after orphans and widows in their distress and to keep oneself from being polluted by the world. James 1:22-27 NIV

Believe it or not—the good news for you is that, in your own strength, you are indeed powerless to be transformed into a righteous being. We are all a mess—all of us. Listen to Isaiah's brief sketch of our problem. He states, *"All of us have become like one who is unclean, and all our righteous acts are like filthy rags; we all shrivel up like a leaf, and like the wind our sins sweep us away."* Isaiah 64:6 NIV

God's laws of love are His promise of how He sees you. He sees you through the lens of your Savior. When He reflects the light that shines from His perfect law onto your heart and into your mind, you are exposed to your great need of the One Who will rescue you, remake you and redeem you from the darkness

If you allow Him, He will continue to draw you into the light and increasingly empower you to live fruitfully under His laws of love and their guiding principles. Then your joy will be complete.

Your conscience draws you toward obedience, as God's Spirit invites you into the light and inspires you to live a righteous life. Your inborn rebellious nature pulls you toward the dark side.

This battle within—this violent tug-of-war between the light and the darkness—is your dilemma. You were born fallen, but you can be reborn to arise—new! You can be restored and renewed. You can be rewired! You can become the new you!

This is done by continually surrendering your self-centered, fearful, powerless, heart to the God of light.

Never forget that God is not to blame for the darkness that brings discord and suffering to your world. God wants to lift you above the dreary world of self-centered fear. He longs for you to understand and realize the extreme joys and benefits associated with living under His guiding laws of love.

Satan's rebellious course rails against God's laws of love. He doesn't want you to know the tremendous power, rewards and blessings that come to you when God fills your heart and mind with His perfecting grace. Many who profess to share the Gospel will tell you that the law no longer matters. They will say that you are under grace now—not the law. Well my friend, since Adam

Chapter Twelve / How Do I Look?

and Eve's fall—every redeemed soul has been saved solely by God's benevolent and abundant grace. God's grace draws you into the light of life and empowers you to live free from rebellion against His laws of love and liberty.

Why would you want to give away God's greatest blessings? Why surrender His richest rewards? His laws of love, written on your heart and mind, will bring you into unblemished communion with Him. Satan's and his evil followers desire to steal from you, to kill you and to destroy your every hope. Don't give away your inheritance to that snake.

When someone tells you the law has been done away with, ask them which law. Was it the sanctuary, ceremonial laws that Jesus fulfilled at the cross or the moral law? Ask them what they are talking about? Do they mean we no longer offer animal sacrifices that point to the Lamb of God? Or do them mean it is now okay to murder, steal, commit adultery, lie, worship idols and covet our neighbors spouse, children and possessions?

Jesus spoke often and clearly about the incredible promises wrapped in the inherent and intrinsic gifts freely granted to the citizens of God's kingdom. His citizens are precious vessels containing His sweet abiding presence. They walk in the refreshing light of His perfect laws of love. Jesus said,

> *Do not think that I have come to abolish the Law or the Prophets; I have not come to abolish them but to fulfill them. For truly I tell you, until heaven and earth disappear, not the smallest letter, not the least stroke of a pen, will by any means disappear from the Law until everything is accomplished.*
>
> *Therefore anyone who sets aside one of the least of these commands and teaches others accordingly will be called least in the kingdom of heaven, but whoever practices and teaches these commands will be called great in the kingdom of heaven.*
>
> *For I tell you that unless your righteousness surpasses that of the Pharisees and the teachers of the law, you will certainly not enter the kingdom of heaven.* Matthew 5: 17-20 NIV

He also said:

As the Father has loved me, so have I loved you. Now remain in my love. If you keep my commands, you will remain in my love, just as I have kept my Father's commands and remain in his love. I have told you this so that my joy may be in you and that your joy may be complete. John 15:8-11 NIV

Don't let that evil snake Satan steal, kill and destroy your complete joy. Allow God to write His laws of love on your heart and in your mind. It is Satan that is behind all the destruction in this world. It all began in the Garden of Eden when he deceived Adam and Eve into believing his lies about God's character and the motives behind His laws of love an liberty. He wants to deceive you into believing that the darkness ruling our world is God's fault. He wants you to blame God. But that's what liars do—they lie.

You are not alone. You have not been left to fend for yourself. Heavenly power is available to you.

The Father, Son and Spirit provide the well-lit Way out of darkness and fear. You too, can be restored to your Creators original design. You too, can walk in love and not fear. You too, can overcome the pain and sorrow of this life. You too, can obey His commands. You too, can realize in increasing measure the completeness of joy that comes to those who walk in the light. You too, can know and follow the Way the Truth and the Life.

Look up and live. Step out of the shadows. Allow the light of God's love to illuminate the darkness and raise you above the noise and distractions of this sin-sick world. It is all yours by faith in the benevolent, saving grace of our Lord and Savior—Jesus Christ and the indwelling, heart-transforming presence of His Holy Spirit.

Chapter Thirteen

John 3:16 — The Way Home

Has your heart been damaged by a distorted belief in the character of God? Does your mind bear the scars of fearful definitions, descriptions and distorted pictures of your perfect, heavenly Father God?

If you are a living, breathing human, chances are that at least some portion of your understanding of God is wrong. It is very likely that your beliefs about many things in this life are incorrect. The enemy has tried desperately to make God appear cold, vengeful and all-together frightening.

The devil's entire rebellion is built upon a foundation of lies. Your world is infested with them. Yet, your darkness can been vanquished by the light.

It is all quite simple and revealed on poster board at nearly every sporting event in the nation. JOHN 3:16

For God so loved the world that he gave his one and only Son, that whoever believes in him shall not perish but have eternal life.

Herein lays the hope for the human race and from this vital verse streams limitless insight into who God is.

Why is it difficult to see God clearly?

Human beings are born into this world with distorted and ungodly motives, affections, desires, feelings and thoughts that lead to actions that bewilder.

Every human heart cries for clarity about this life. All humans are broken. It can be difficult to see God clearly amidst the chaos of life. It is when you do see God clearly and understand the depth of His love and desire for you that you begin to heal.

God is a perfect Father. A father provides discipline from a heart of love and a desire for the best for his children. God can seem to appear harsh in much of the old testament. But in each situation, His apparent harshness can be clearly seen as the discipline and protective care of a loving Father.

If your children were put in a life threatening position and you needed to eliminate an enemy in order to save those children—would you do it?

God knows who will and who won't accept His offer of salvation and restoration. He allows the weeds to grow with the grain—for a time. But when the harvest is threatened, He must act to salvage what He can. The great flood didn't come upon the earth until there was only one man left who sought the Father and His salvation—Noah.

God appears to eliminate large numbers of people at random throughout the old testament. At least until He gets Jesus Christ, our only hope and redeemer, through the battle lines.

There is an unseen battle raging upon the earth. The evil one knew that Jesus was coming to ransom us. He was using every weapon in his arsenal to prevent the eternal hope—Jesus Christ, from completing His mission. As you study the Bible you will notice that there are no mass deaths occurring at the hand of God after Jesus completes His mission.

Perhaps God in His infinite wisdom was allowing the humans that were working under the influence of the enemy of souls to die the first death before they could get in the way of our Savior's arrival. God sees physical death differently than we may. He calls physical death a sleep. He may have allowed some who had determined to reject Him to fall asleep in order to protect those

Chapter Thirteen / John 3:16 — The Way Home

who would accept His gifts. We must place our faith somewhere. Why not in the revealed will and benevolence of our perfect Father God.

He reveals everything clearly in Scripture. He hides nothing from us that we need in order to make informed decisions and find the power to overcome.

God assumes responsibility for everything that happens in His creation. The buck stops with Him.

We may never know why, but God takes responsibility for everything sin has caused. He willingly heaps upon Himself all that is done under the sun.

> *One of the most important messages of the Old Testament sanctuary system is that, though He is not to blame, God takes responsibility for sin. The sanctuary was an invitation for the Israelites to bring their sin to God, knowing that when they approached Him, they would be forgiven.*
>
> *This has always been God's objective in dealing with the sin problem. You see, choosing to sin, immediately injected a fear of God into the hearts of Adam and Eve. But God doesn't want there to be separation between us. Thus, in all things, God has been working to reconcile us to Himself. Through the life and death of Christ, God devoted Himself to that reconciliation for all time. In order to provide the opportunity for reconciliation, God sacrificed Himself— not holding anything back. He took the full weight of our suffering and depravity upon Himself. So, though He was in no way to blame for sin, God took the responsibility of providing a solution.*
>
> *Now we know that we have a helper in God, not an obstacle. We know that we have a friend in God, not an enemy.*
>
> *Instead of leaving us alone in the darkness of our sin, God entered our disordered world and sacrificed Himself to present us with the gift of salvation.* Fundamental Focus

At the base of every uncomfortable action displayed for all to see on the pages of the Bible, you will find love. God is love. Wisdom will place faith in Him. We build our faith upon hearing the word of God. *"So then faith comes by hearing, and hearing by the word of God."* Romans 10:17 NKJV

Faith is supported by God's revelations of Himself as disclosed in the Bible. You should study the Scriptures for yourself. There are messages of love there for all mankind and there are messages of love there for you personally. Don't rob yourself of the power, direction and wisdom revealed on the pages of the most valuable, book ever put together. Can you trust the Bible? We believe you can.

Erwin Lutzer wrote an enlightened book on why you can trust the Bible, entitled, <u>Seven Reasons Why You Can Trust the Bible</u>.

They are:
1.) A logical Reason—The Claims of the Bible
2.) A Historical Reason—The Reliability of the Bible
3.) A Prophetic Reason—The Predictions of the Bible
4.) A Christological Reason—The Authority of Christ
5.) A Scientific Reason—The Story of Creation
6.) A Providential Reason—The Canonical Reason
7.) A Personal Reason—The Power of the Word [c]

Your God, and Satan's rebellion against Him, is exposed on the pages of the written Word. God has delivered the entire story of this broken world in the Scriptures—from the fall—to the eternal life that follows, for those who accept the salvation He has provided. Scripture not only reveals Satan as the deceiver and responsible party behind the devastation that plagues your soul, it also reveals your heavenly Father's true character.

The following list includes some of the definitions of God as revealed in His written word, as well as some of His precious gifts and core character traits:

I am the first and the last, the Alpha and the Omega, the Beginning and the End.[1] *Without Me you can do nothing.*[2] *With Me you can do all things.*[3] *I am the Spirit of the Universe, the Creator of all there is.*[4] *I am Immanuel.*[5] *I am All and in all.*[6] *I am the Breath of Life.*[7] *I am the Source of all Wisdom, Knowledge and Understanding.*[8] *I am your Strength and your Shield.*[9] *I am your Hope.*[10] *I am your Brother.*[11] *I am a Consuming Fire.*[12] *I am your Ransom.*[13] *I am*

Chapter Thirteen / John 3:16 — The Way Home

your Redeemer.[14] I am your Savior.[15] I am the Root and the Offspring of David the Bright Morning Star.[16] I am the Son of Man.[17] I am the Son of God.[18] I am the God who Justifies.[19] I am the Lord of Hosts.[20] I am the King of kings.[21] I am the Lord your God.[22] I am your Friend.[23] I am Jealous over you.[24] I am the Way, the Truth and the Life.[25] I am the Lord Almighty.[26] I am the Good Shepherd.[27] I am the Lamb of God.[28] I am the Resurrection and the Life.[29] I am your Judge.[30] I am your Mediator.[31] I am the Wonderful Counselor, Mighty God, Everlasting Father, Prince of Peace.[32] I am your Advocate.[33] I am the Lord of lords.[34] I am the Head of the Church. I am the Faithful and True Witness. I am your Salvation.[35] I am your Master.[36] I am your High Priest.[37] I am the Gate.[38] I am the Living Water.[39] I am the Bread of Life.[40] I am your Shield, your Fortress and your High Tower.[41] I am the True Vine.[42] I am the Messiah.[43] I am the Man of Sorrows.[44] I am the Holy One.[45] I am the Beloved Son.[46] I am the Branch.[47] I am the Light of the World.[48] I am the Image of the Invisible God.[49] I am the Word.[50] I am the Chief Cornerstone.[51] I am the Servant.[52] I am the Rock.[53] I am the Author and Finisher of your Faith.[54] I am the Pearl of Great Price.[55] I am Jacob's Ladder.[56] I am the Lion of the Tribe of Judah.[57] I am the only Begotten Son.[58] I am the Bridegroom.[59] I am your Surety.[60] I am the Spirit of Creation.[61] I am the Comforter.[62] I am the Helper.[63] I Am that I Am.[64] I am the Firstborn over all Creation.[65] I am the Lord, the Compassionate and Gracious God, slow to anger, abounding in love and faithfulness, maintaining love to thousands, and forgiving wickedness, rebellion and sin.[66] I am your Substitute.[67]

    I am Light.[68] I am Love.[69] I am the Teacher.[70] D*

God, in Christ, has all authority and power in heaven and on earth. Mat 28:18 NIV

*(See Notes Section for Bible verse references)

God has all power, all wisdom and all knowledge. He knows how to heal, repair, restore, rewire and inspire you.

A primary goal of this book is not only to expose a clearer

vision of God and His true character, but to demonstrate how much He desires to recreate and redeem you. Please let Him.

For more information on how to allow God to transform you by the renewing of your mind, you may wish to obtain a copy of our book—God, Please Rewire My MADFATs.

We spent decades researching Scripture and Neuroscience, as well as Christian Counseling and Coaching techniques.

As a result of this research a God-inspired system for success was revealed to us that truly helps create an environment within the human heart where God's Holy Spirit can transform your broken soul by the renewing of your mind.

This system for success is available to you in our book entitled, *Health and Happiness in a Broken World.* You can get a copy from our website ExploringGodsLove.com.

Chapter Fourteen

Promises

I am often awakened in the deep of the night. While sleeping soundly, dreaming my little dreams—He comes. His words vibrating in my soul, "I have a mission, a matter of universal interest. I want you to use your voice to share my love with others."

He prepared me for this time. All of my study, all of my struggles, all of my experience in the war between good and evil has been a training ground for this mission.

When He calls, I rise from my slumber and sit – listening. Waiting for inspiration. Ready to take dictation. Then, He enlightens my mind with His thoughts, His words, His vision for you and for me. Urgent messages for all who have ears to hear.

He wants us to grasp the deep realities of what is in truly in store for those who choose Him.

The Holy Scriptures are packaged in promise. All of the Father's promises are ours, in the gift of His willing sacrifice for us, in His Son – Jesus Christ.

These are some of the rights, gifts and privileges of those who accept and obey Him. The benefits of being adopted into God's royal family.

His sure promises include:

Eternal life, *"For this is how God loved the world: He gave his one and only Son, so that everyone who believes in him will not perish but have eternal life."* John 3:16 NLT

Freedom from slavery to a defective character, *"It was for freedom that Christ set us free; therefore keep standing firm and do not be subject again to a yoke of slavery."* Galatians 5:1 NASB

A life filled with the fruit of God's Spirit, *"love, joy, peace, patience, kindness, goodness, faithfulness, gentleness, and self-control."* Galatians 5:22-23 NLT

Freedom, insight and God's favor, *"The Spirit of the Lord is upon me, for he has anointed me to bring Good News to the poor. He has sent me to proclaim that captives will be released, that the blind will see, that the oppressed will be set free, and that the time of the Lord's favor has come."* Luke 4:18-19 NLT

Everything you touch will prosper, *"The Lord your God will then make you successful in everything you do. He will give you many children and numerous livestock, and he will cause your fields to produce abundant harvests, for the Lord will again delight in being good to you as he was to your ancestors. The Lord your God will delight in you if you obey his voice and keep the commands and decrees written in this Book of Instruction, and if you turn to the Lord your God with all your heart and soul."* Deuteronomy 30:9-10 NLT

You will have victory over self, *"He who finds his life will lose it, and he who loses his life for My sake will find it."* Matthew 10:39 NASB

He will create in you a new heart. *"Then I will sprinkle clean water on you, and you will be clean; I will cleanse you from all your filthiness and from all your idols. Moreover, I will give you a new heart and put a new spirit within you; and I will remove the heart of stone from your flesh and give you a heart of flesh. I will put My Spirit within you and cause you to walk in My statutes, and you will be careful to observe My ordinances."* Ezekiel 36:25-27 NASB

He will write His Laws on your heart and in your mind, *"I will put my law in their minds and write it on their hearts. I will be their God, and they will be my people"* Jeremiah 31:33 NASB

Chapter Fourteen / *Promises*

Purity of thought and action are yours. *"And now, dear brothers and sisters, one final thing. Fix your thoughts on what is true, and honorable, and right, and pure, and lovely, and admirable. Think about things that are excellent and worthy of praise."* Philippians 4:8 NLT

You shall not want. *"The Lord is my shepherd; I shall not want."* Psalm 23:1 NKJV

Your shepherd has given His life for you, *"I am the good shepherd. The good shepherd gives His life for the sheep."* John 10:11 NKJV

He will be your fortress, your shield, your stronghold, your strength, your rock, *"I will love You, O Lord, my strength. The Lord is my rock and my fortress and my deliverer; My God, my strength, in whom I will trust; My shield and the horn of my salvation, my stronghold."* Psalm 18:1-2 NKJV

You will be in good health and prosper, *"Beloved, I pray that you may prosper in all things and be in health, just as your soul prospers."* 3 John 2 NKJV

He will never leave you or abandon you, *"No, I will not abandon you as orphans—I will come to you."* John 14:18 NLT

He will give you abundant life, *"The thief does not come except to steal, and to kill, and to destroy. I have come that they may have life, and that they may have it more abundantly."* John 10:10 NKJV

He will restore your soul, *"He makes me to lie down in green pastures; He leads me beside the still waters. He restores my soul; He leads me in the paths of righteousness for His name's sake."* Psalm 23:2-3 NKJV

You will seek Him and you will find Him, when you seek Him with all of your heart, *"And you will seek Me and find Me, when you search for Me with all your heart."* Jeremiah 29:13 NKJV

His Spirit will dwell in you, *"If you love Me, keep My commandments. And I will pray the Father, and He will give you another Helper, that He may abide with you forever—the Spirit of truth, whom the world cannot receive, because it neither sees Him nor knows Him; but you know Him, for He dwells with you and will be in you."* John 14:15-17 NKJV

His Word will be a light on your path, *"Your word is a lamp to my feet and a light to my path."* Psalm 119:105 NKJV

Super-natural blessings and rewards will come to you,
"Blessed are the poor in spirit, for theirs is the kingdom of heaven.

Blessed are those who mourn, for they shall be comforted.

Blessed are the meek, for they shall inherit the earth.

Blessed are those who hunger and thirst for righteousness, for they shall be filled.

Blessed are the merciful, for they shall obtain mercy.

Blessed are the pure in heart, for they shall see God.

Blessed are the peacemakers, for they shall be called sons of God.

Blessed are those who are persecuted for righteousness' sake, for theirs is the kingdom of heaven.

Blessed are you when they revile and persecute you, and say all kinds of evil against you falsely for My sake. Rejoice and be exceedingly glad, for great is your reward in heaven, for so they persecuted the prophets who were before you." Matthew 5:3-12 NKJV

You will know peace amidst the chaos, *"These things I have spoken to you, so that in Me you may have peace. In the world you have tribulation, but take courage; I have overcome the world."* John 16:33 NASB

You will rejoice in trials, *"Dear brothers and sisters, when troubles of any kind come your way, consider it an opportunity for great joy. For you know that when your faith is tested, your endurance has a chance to grow. So let it grow, for when your endurance is fully developed, you will be perfect and complete, needing nothing."* James 1:2-4 NLT

The Father will discipline you as His child, *"As you endure this divine discipline, remember that God is treating you as his own children. Who ever heard of a child who is never disciplined by its father?"* Hebrews 12:7 NLT

He has given you everything you need to live a godly life, *"His divine power has given us everything we need for a godly life through our knowledge of him who called us by his own glory and goodness."* 2 Peter 1:3 NIV

You need not fear the darkness, *"Even though I walk through the darkest valley, I will fear no evil, for you are with me; your rod and your staff, they comfort me."* Psalm 23:4 NIV

Chapter Fourteen / Promises

You will reap what you sow, *"Do not be deceived, God is not mocked; for whatever a man sows, that he will also reap."* Galatians 6:7 NKJV

You have hope of renewal in a dying body, *"That is why we never give up. Though our bodies are dying, our spirits are being renewed every day."* 2 Corinthians 4:16 NLT

You will receive a new body, *"And we believers also groan, even though we have the Holy Spirit within us as a foretaste of future glory, for we long for our bodies to be released from sin and suffering. We, too, wait with eager hope for the day when God will give us our full rights as his adopted children, including the new bodies he has promised us."* Romans 8:23 NLT

Even though you were born into rebellion God will grant you eternal life, *"For the wages of sin is death, but the free gift of God is eternal life through Christ Jesus our Lord."* Romans 6:23 NLT

Your sins are thrown into the depths of the ocean, *"Once again you will have compassion on us. You will trample our sins under your feet and throw them into the depths of the ocean!"* Micah 7:19 NLT

God is your compassionate, forgiving Father, *"He does not punish us for all our sins; he does not deal harshly with us, as we deserve. For his unfailing love toward those who fear him is as great as the height of the heavens above the earth. He has removed our sins as far from us as the east is from the west. The Lord is like a father to his children, tender and compassionate to those who fear him. For he knows how weak we are; he remembers we are only dust."* Psalm 103:1014 NLT

You have an advocate against the evil one who accuses you before God, *"My dear children, I am writing this to you so that you will not sin. But if anyone does sin, we have an advocate who pleads our case before the Father. He is Jesus Christ, the one who is truly righteous. He himself is the sacrifice that atones for our sins—and not only our sins but the sins of all the world."* 1 John 2:1-2 NLT

You will be increasingly transformed into God's image, *"But we all, with unveiled face, beholding as in a mirror the glory of the Lord, are being transformed into the same image from glory to glory, just as by the Spirit of the Lord."* 2 Corinthians 7:18 NKJV

You are God's friend, *"No longer do I call you servants, for a servant does not know what his master is doing; but I have called*

you friends, for all things that I heard from My Father I have made known to you." John 15:15 NKJV

Once this dark story is over, there will never again be anyone who will wish to usurp the Father's government. We will know the results of choosing to stray from His perfect Laws of Love. We will desire only the best for ourselves as well as any and all other beings. We delight in doing His will for we know that it is the very best that can ever be.

We will all trust in the Lord and not our own understanding, *"Trust in the Lord with all your heart, and lean not on your own understanding; In all your ways acknowledge Him, and He shall direct your paths."* Proverbs 3:5-6 NKJV

We hope that you have chosen to walk with us as we strive to know and to follow the Way back home to our happy beginnings. Our greatest longing is to travel deep into the outer reaches of God's vast, ever-expanding universe and continually discover its incredibly awe-inspiring treasures with the Father, the Son, the Spirit and you.

Until then, *"May the Lord bless you and protect you. May the Lord smile on you and be gracious to you. May the Lord show you his favor and give you his peace."* Numbers 6:24-26 NLT

James Bars

Chapter One / *Who Is Your God? And, Why the Chaos?*

Notes:

1. Revelation 22:13 TNIV
2. John 15:5 TNIV
3. Philippians 4:13 TNIV
4. Genesis 1:1-2 TNIV
5. Matthew 1:23 NKJV
6. Colossians 1:15-19 TNIV
7. Genesis 2:7 NIV
8. Proverbs 2:6 TNIV
9. Psalm 28:7 TNIV
10. 1 Timothy 4:10 TNIV
11. Matthew 12:50 TNIV
12. Hebrews 12:29 TNIV
13. 1 Timothy 2:5-6 TNIV
14. Isaiah 44:6 TNIV
15. Titus 2:13 TNIV
16. Revelation 22:16 TNIV
17. Mark 2:10 TNIV
18. Matthew 16:16 TNIV
19. Romans 4:5 TNIV
20. Jeremiah 7:3 NKJV
21. Revelation 17:14 TNIV
22. Exodus 20:2 TNIV
23. John 15:15 TNIV
24. Exodus 20:5 TNIV
25. John 14:6 TNIV
26. Isaiah 44:6 TNIV
27. John 10:14 TNIV
28. John 1:29 TNIV
29. John 11:25 TNIV
30. 2 Timothy 4:1 TNIV
31. 1 Timothy 2:5 TNIV
32. Isaiah 9:6 TNIV
33. 1 John 2:1 TNIV
34. 1 Timothy 6:15 TNIV
35. Ephesians 5:23 TNIV
36. Luke 17:13 TNIV
37. Hebrews 3:1 TNIV
38. John 10:7 TNIV
39. John 4:13 TNIV
40. John 6:35 TNIV
41. Psalm 144:2 NKJV
42. John 15:1 TNIV
43. Matthew 16:16 TNIV
44. Isaiah 53:3 NKJV
45. John 6:69 TNIV
46. Matthew 3:17 NKJV
47. Jeremiah 23:5 TNIV
48. John 8:12 TNIV
49. Colossians 1:15 TNIV
50. John 1:1 TNIV
51. Luke 20:17 TNIV
52. Mark 10:45 TNIV
53. Psalm 18:46 TNIV
54. Hebrews 12:2 NKJV
55. Matthew 13:46 NKJV
56. Genesis 28:12 NKJV
57. Revelation 5:5 NKJV
58. John 3:16 NKJV
59. John 2:9 NKJV
60. Hebrews 7:22 NKJV
61. Genesis 1:1 NKJV
62. John 15:26 KJV
63. John 15:26 NKJV
64. Exodus 3:14 NKJV
65. Colossians 1:15 NKJV
66. Exodus 34:6-7 TNIV
67. Romans 6:23-24 TNIV
68. 1 John 1:5 TNIV
69. 1 John 4:8 TNIV
70. John 13:13 TNIV

[71] John 14:15 TNIV
[72] Exodus 20: 1:17 TNIV
[73] Jeremiah 31:33 TNIV
[74] Psalm 19:7-11 TNIV
[75] Ezekiel 36:26-27 NLT
[76] Jeremiah 31:33 TNIV
[77] Romans 12:2 TNIV

The heavens declare the glory of God;

the skies proclaim the work of his hands.

Day after day they pour forth speech;

night after night they reveal knowledge.

They have no speech, they use no words; no sound is heard from them.

Yet their voice goes out into all the earth,

their words to the ends of the world. _{Psalm 19:1-4 NIV}

Exploring God's Love
Daily Nurture and Endless Healing in Heaven's Light

Most people desire to know safety, to belong, and to matter.
Living as an expression of God's love is the surest path to realizing your heart's desires.
It is daily nurture that enables your spirit to walk in His ways!
This engaging, love-based treatise, unites ancient light from God's word with current science to steadily nurture and heal every facet of your being.
You will know safety in Heaven's light, you will realize absolute belonging as God's beloved, and you will truly matter as an ambassador of His kingdom of love.
On your adventure, you will enjoy space to daily journal your discoveries and desires.
Your joy awaits!

This book contains much of the same material as *God, Please Rewire My MADFATs*. But is presented in a more easily absorbed format and includes space to journal your daily discoveries and desires.

$14.95 US and Canada

Available at Amazon.com
and ExploringGodsLove.com

Recovery Journal
Laugh, Learn, Pray, Affirm

Second Edition

Journal: A personal record of intimate communion, inquiry, and reflection.
Journey: A passage from one place to another.
This book is both.
It will prove fruitful for any seeker, especially those in recovery from addiction and co-dependency.
This playful and enlightening, spiritual quest will add color to the rich horizons of your renewing mind.
You will smile and laugh.
Your meditations will enlighten the sage inside you and brighten barricaded gardens in your soul.
Your aspiring prayers will vitalize the kingdom of God that lies within.
You will affirm your intrinsic value as heaven's child.
Your wisdom, knowledge, and understanding will strengthen.
Your hope will flourish within God's promises.
You will know the Way to your divine Father's welcoming home.

Available at Amazon.com
and ExploringGodsLove.com

Whose Are You?

Join us as we travel back through the travail of millenniums to a galaxy far, far away.

Witness the birth of darkness. Be there as our Liberator begins His counter-intuitive and radically irreligious war for universal dominion and each living soul's allegiance.

Discover the Spirit, the Way and the true story behind the veil of History.

ISBN: 978-0-9817534-0-9 $9.95

Available at *Amazon.com*
and *ExploringGodsLove.com*

The Nourished Soul ~ Nurturing Your Mind to Grow Unending Health and Happiness

"More than anything you guard, protect your mind, for life flows from it." Proverbs 4:23 CEB

The incomprehensible powers and abilities of your brain are without equal among earth's other organisms. Your mind is your brain in action. Whoever you become here and hereafter will be determined by the choices you make with your mind. Love or fear will dominate your thought life. You decide which one gets fed.

Love and its flourishing manifestations of joy, peace, patience, kindness, goodness, faithfulness, gentleness, and self-control will envelop your heart, when practiced, and leave you pleasantly fulfilled and content. Healthy love relaxes your limbic system, counters the effects of fear, and assists you in the expansion of positive, uplifting abilities.

As you free love—love will free you. Developing tangible, well-practiced, alternative neural pathways of love and care will override your inherited and cultivated neural pathways of fear and selfishness, and you will begin to enjoy life like never before.

"If you can change your mind, you can change your life." — William James

Available at Amazon.com
and ExploringGodsLove.com

Booklets:

It's All In Your Mind
Summary of Chapter 1 of
The Nourished Soul

The Spirit's Song
Summary of Chapters 4 & 5 of
The Nourished Soul

The Way Up
Summary of Chapter 6 of
The Nourished Soul

Untangling the Night
Summary of Chapter 7 of
The Nourished Soul

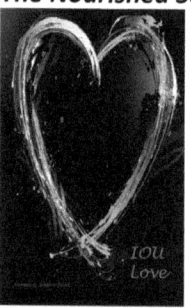

IOU Love
Summary of Chapter 8 of
The Nourished Soul

Happy You,
In God's Temple of Light
Summary of Chapter 9 of
The Nourished Soul

www.ingramcontent.com/pod-product-compliance
Lightning Source LLC
Chambersburg PA
CBHW071414040426
42444CB00009B/2240